MOTIVICSOLOING FORJAZZBASS

Learn to Build Melodic Solos & Grooving Basslines With Simple Motifs

CHRISMINHDOKY

FUNDAMENTALCHANGES

Motivic Soloing for Jazz Bass

Learn to Build Melodic Solos & Grooving Basslines With Simple Motifs

ISBN: 978-1-78933-424-1

Published by **www.fundamental-changes.com**

Copyright © 2025 Chris Minh Doky

Edited by Tim Pettingale

www.fundamental-changes.com

@fundamentalchanges

Join our free Facebook Community of Cool Musicians

www.facebook.com/groups/fundamentalguitar

Contents

Introduction

Of course, I'm biased, but I truly believe that the best spot on the stage is the bass player's chair. Why? Because the bass is an essential part of the groove, but bassists also have a role to play in dictating the harmony and the overall vibe of the music. Personally, that's what I love so much about playing bass – we get to be involved in *every* aspect of the music.

My understanding of the bass player's role is that we should do everything we can to facilitate an environment in which the other band members can thrive and sound their best. The bass should support everyone else in the band, and be the glue between the rhythm (which we take care of in partnership with the drums) and the harmony.

This might sound like an odd statement, but we must not forget that the role of the bass player is to play the *bass*! In other words, our primary task is to hold down the bottom end. It's always fun to play solos, but for the majority of the time, in any live situation, we need to go downtown and play those low notes – making sure they're the right notes, and in the right place!

I like to think of the drums as the heartbeat of the band and the bass as the lungs. As bass players, it's our job to make the music breathe, both rhythmically and harmonically. In this book, we'll explore lots of different ways in which you can do that, and look at a range of techniques you can use to create solid basslines.

In my bass playing, I've always gravitated towards melodic storytelling, coupled with a desire to create organic, expressive lines. That's true whether I'm holding down a groove or improvising a solo, and one of the greatest tools I've found to facilitate this approach is the *motif*.

Simply put, a motif is a short melodic idea that can be repeated and adapted. A motif may last for a bar or two before being replaced by a new idea, or it can become the theme of an entire chapter of your solo. I also hold the belief that motifs are not *just* for soloing – we can use them to develop our bottom end grooves too.

So, in this book I want to teach you how to create unlimited bassline and soloing ideas from motival ideas. Once you get into the idea, you'll fall in love with the fact that you can start with something pretty simple, then take it and develop it in endless ways. This way of approaching the bass is highly creative as well as melodic, and I trust it will grow your bass playing in ways you didn't expect.

Enjoy the journey!

Chris.

Get the Audio

The audio files for this book are available to download for free from **www.fundamental-changes.com.** The link is in the top right-hand corner. Click on the "Bass" link then simply select this book title from the drop-down menu and follow the instructions to get the audio.

We recommend that you download the files directly to your computer, not to your tablet, and extract them there before adding them to your media library. You can then put them onto your tablet, iPod or burn them to CD. On the download page there are instructions and we also provide technical support via the contact form.

Join our free Facebook Community of Cool Musicians

www.facebook.com/groups/fundamentalguitar

Tag us for a share on Instagram: **FundamentalChanges**

Chapter One – The Foundations of Groove

The role of every bass player is to add groove or swing to the music. It doesn't matter whether you're playing funk, jazz, rock, or even classical music – the music has got to "groove" rhythmically, and the bass plays a key role in making that happen.

Bass players use the term *groove* or *swing* as a way of describing the physical feeling that good music creates – because a great groove is something we can feel in our gut. It could be a funky thing, a swinging jazz groove, or a piece of Mozart – if it's played right, it'll groove.

We can all hear the difference between a bassist who is just playing the notes and one who is grooving in the pocket of the time, so that it makes us want to move in response. The question is, how can we learn to *swing* when we play? For clarity, I don't just mean playing in time – I mean creating a swing feel that is appropriate to the language of the song. We'll explore the answer to that in this chapter and I'll pass on my thoughts on how to develop this skill.

One very important lesson I learned as a bass player is that we first need to be able to function as a bassist *on our own,* before we add the complication of playing with other musicians. We can't be the glue that holds the band together if we don't have good time within ourselves.

For that reason, I teach all of my students to become "self-sustaining" musicians. In other words, they need to be able to keep excellent time and create a groove just by themselves, without any outside elements to interact with. We're going to work on that skill now, because developing it will create a great foundation for your bass playing.

The first and most obvious way to develop your inner sense of time is by working with a metronome. This might initially sound a bit boring, but it can become a much more engaging process when our goal is to make the metronome *swing*. Let's look at how we can make that happen.

Making the Metronome Groove

Most modern styles of music developed out of blues and jazz. In jazz, it's common to play with a two-beat feel to create a simple swing feel. This means playing just two 1/4 notes per 4/4 measure and placing them on beats 1 and 3.

Whatever style of music you gravitate towards, practicing grooving with just two 1/4 notes will help you to develop your sense of time and give you a solid foundation on which you can then build musical ideas.

Here's how it sounds played over a Dm7 chord. In this example, I'm deliberately choking the 1/4 notes so that they sustain for less than their full note value. This immediately creates a simple groove because we can clearly hear the metronome click when we're not playing, and shortening the 1/4 notes gives the music a little more space.

Example 1a

1/4 notes mostly played shorter than their full value

This is not the most exciting bassline you'll ever play, but it serves to illustrate the simplest form of the two-beat groove. The aim is to play on beats 1 and 3 and always hit an important note (i.e., a chord tone) when doing so.

We're playing over a Dm7 harmony, so we could choose to play the root note, the b3, the 5th or the b7. Here I'm playing just the root (D) and 5th (A) of the Dm7 chord and moving the 5th up and down the octave.

We need to play the root note to define the harmony, and since we only have one other note to play, the 5th is a good choice because it's a "solid" note that grounds the harmony, and clearly points to the "1", in other words, making the chords breath. This is the very basic starting point of selecting notes for our bassline.

Staying with this simple root and 5th approach, let's start to make this bassline groove.

When I teach this to students, I tell them to think less about themselves and more about what's outside of them. As bass players we should think of ourselves as facilitators of the groove – the element of the music that works with the tempo to make it swing – and making the music groove is the most important function of the bass.

By itself, the metronome doesn't swing – it's perfectly constant – so how can we make it sound like it's grooving?

We can achieve this by subtly *pushing* and *pulling* the time around it. We do this by controlling the length of the notes we play and also by introducing a percussive element where we play *ghost notes* or *dead notes*. Ghost notes are played by gently tapping the fretboard, sometimes sounding an actual note and other times just producing a percussive hit.

Have a listen to the audio of Example 1b. In the first half of the recording. I'm deliberately playing straight and not trying to make the metronome swing.

In the second half, I'm controlling the note lengths and introducing some ghost note taps on the fretboard. In the notation below these are indicated with an X, which means that the string should be muted. Just lift the fingers of your fretting hand very slightly to mute the strings as you tap the fretboard with your plucking hand.

Example 1b

1/4 notes mostly played shorter than their full value

In the second half of Example 1b, I played the same chord tones as before, but anticipated certain notes with ghost notes.

In bar two, the ghost note that anticipates the A note on the top string is an 1/8th note. We count 1/8th notes in a bar by saying, "1 & 2 & 3 & 4 &". This ghost note falls on the & of beat 2, and this creates a slight *push* in the groove.

In bar three, we move the ghost note to beat 4&, so that it falls right at the end of the bar and anticipates the root note that is played on beat 1 of bar four. Doing this gives the note on beat 1 more gravity than if we played it straight.

In bar four, the ghost note falls in the same place as bar two, on the 2&.

What's happening here is that we're helping the music to *breathe*. We're still holding down the groove by playing on beats 1 and 3 but we're also introducing the push and pull that makes the metronome sound like it's swinging.

This is the first step in creating a groove.

In the introduction, I mentioned that there are two ways in which we can affect the groove and feel of the music: *rhythmically* and *harmonically*. Let's dig deeper into that.

Rhythm

Let's look at how altering our rhythmic phrasing affects the groove. We began by adding ghost notes into our bassline. One way of thinking about these ghost notes is that they hint at directions in which we can take the music, if we were to play real notes.

Example 1c illustrates this idea, showing how we can alter our phrasing to create a more interesting bassline, while still preserving the main pulse of the groove. There are still some ghost notes here, but they are played very quietly. Check out the audio to hear the exact articulation.

In bar one, we hit chord tones on beats 1 and 3, then repeat the A note on beat 4&. This serves the same purpose as the ghost note in bar three of the previous example – to anticipate the note on beat 1 of bar two and highlight it.

In bar two, we hit the 5th on beat 3 as expected, but this time play it as part of a phrase. The phrasing idea is to play the 5th (A) up and down the octave, separated by another note.

The "other" note here is an extended chord tone (E), with is the 9th of the Dm7 chord. This note bridges the gap between the A octave notes. Notice here that the two 1/8th notes are followed by a 1/4 note. The longer 1/4 note creates a slight *pull* on the groove.

Bar three reverts to the straight two-beat feel, but in bar four we omit the note on beat 3 and play it on beat 3& instead. This rhythmic displacement idea also creates a pull against the rigid tempo of the metronome, causing it to swing.

Bars 5-8 use similar phrasing ideas to create the swing feel.

Example 1c

Everything we play on the bass should serve the purpose of showing what's coming up next. We can create a little bit of excitement or tension by not playing on the expected beats (1 and 3), and when we do bring it home, those solid notes are emphasized all the more.

This is all part of learning to make the music breathe. We can add in creative phrases to make our basslines more interesting, but at the same time still make it clear where the 1 is, and signal to our bandmates where the groove is heading.

Harmony

The second way we can affect the groove is harmonically. Breaking away from the strict root and 5th pattern, we can begin to elaborate on our bassline by introducing other chord tones or approach notes.

Here's an example that starts with the familiar root and 5th pattern (applying some of the rhythmic ideas we've discussed so far), and is then embellished with other notes and rhythmic phrases.

Let's break down what's happening.

In bar two, the A note on beat 3 is played staccato, which subtly alters the phrasing and its effect on the groove.

Bar four includes the E note we introduced earlier (9th of Dm7), but we place an Eb approach note before it. Approach notes are common in jazz. It just means to play a note a half step below or above a chord tone. Sometimes the approach note may be a scale tone and sometimes a *chromatic* note i.e., a note that doesn't belong to the key. The latter is the case here.

Also notice that the chromatic Eb note falls on beat 3 of the bar, then slides into the E. This is another technique used frequently in jazz. Normally, we want to play chord tones on the strong beats of the bar to anchor the harmony, but placing a chromatic passing note on a strong beat creates a moment of tension that is then resolved.

Bar six features another chromatic phrase. In this bar, we're hitting the D root note and the A (5th) on beats 1 and 3, but we approach the A note from two frets below and include a chromatic approach note. This phrase starts on a G note (the 11th of Dm7), then plays a chromatic Ab note, then the A. It's an example of *chord tone targeting*.

This just means that we have a specific chord tone in mind that we want to play on a strong beat of the bar, and we target it with approach notes. Jazz musicians often use multiple approach notes and, despite those notes being outside the harmony, if they hit a chord tone on a strong beat, our ears just accept the outside notes.

In bar eight, we play an entire rhythmic phrase, but it is "enclosed" by bars seven and nine, which are played straight. This is a great way of spelling out the harmony while adding some excitement to the groove by way of contrast.

In bar ten, the root and 5th are on beats 1 and 3 again, but the 5th is wrapped up in a rhythmic phrase.

Example 1d

Listen to the audio and you'll hear that the previous example was swung with an 1/8th note triplet feel, but we can also play with a straight 1/8th note feel and still use ghost notes and phrasing ideas to make the music breathe. Here's an example of that approach.

You'll see that we begin by placing the root and 5th on beats 1 and 3 as before, with the 5th accentuated by placing a ghost note before it.

In bar three, we introduce a rhythmic idea to break up the pattern and also change up the note choices. Here we place an F (the b3 of Dm7) on beat 3. You could view this four-note phrase as targeting the A note on the top string, 2nd fret.

The F note is a dotted 1/8th note, which means it is held for the length of a regular 1/8th note plus half as long again. This is followed by a quick 1/16th note and two more 1/8th notes. The overall effect here is to create a quicker phrase that lands on the root note on beat 1 of bar four.

Notice in bar four that we use a phrase that includes a C note, the b7 of Dm7. The b7 note is used to good effect in bar five also, where we use it to create a motif-like phrase. This is followed by some space at the beginning of bar six, and is a good example of allowing the music to breathe by controlling the length of our notes and sometimes leaving an empty space for other instruments to fill.

In bar seven, the motif stated in bar five is repeated, but played on the A string rather than the open D string, with added articulation. Bars 5-8 are like a question and answer phrase. The question is stated twice and answered differently each time.

Example 1e

The previous example introduced some different note choices we can make over this simple D minor groove.

The first thing to say about that is, it's important we don't get caught up thinking too much about note choices and forget our main objective: to make the metronome groove.

Secondly, whatever we play, rhythmically or harmonically, has to be clear to our fellow musicians, so that we all know where we're going. We don't want to play rhythmic figures that don't lead anywhere or notes that don't make sense over the harmony. Our job is to lead the way for the rest of the band by laying a firm foundation.

With these principles in mind, let's look at how we can develop our palette of notes and apply different rhythms to move our bassline forward. We'll explore several different ideas through three 16-bar examples.

First, here is sixteen bars of jamming over a Dm7 chord. This will sound pretty busy, but there's only a metronome and me at this stage. I won't analyze every single idea here, as you can probably work them out for yourself, but I'll highlight a couple of things.

Bars 1-3 use a motif idea, stated in bar one then adapted, which goes root, 5th, b7, root. We can take a simple idea like this and just keep developing it with different rhythmic placements.

In bar four we break up this idea with a five-note phrase using the D Blues scale (D, F, G, Ab, A, C). The C and Db notes at the end of the bar are approach notes, targeting the D root note that falls on beat 1 of bar five.

In bars 5-7 we return to the original motif, then add a fill in bar eight. Although this phrase definitely sounds bluesy, there's no "blue note" here (i.e., the b5, Ab). The notes come from the D Minor Pentatonic scale (D, F, G, A, C).

The fill in bar twelve plays C octaves (the b7 of Dm7), then shifts up to Db as a way of approaching the D root note in the next bar.

Example 1f

We began this chapter with a very simple bassline, and we've gradually developed it into something altogether more complex. We still need to keep in mind that our role in any musical setting is to support the other musicians. We'll get our chance to take a solo, but for the majority of the time, our role on the bandstand is to *be* the groove and the *breath* of the music.

We began by playing just the root and 5th on beats 1 and 3. We can embellish those notes, sometimes miss them out, apply different rhythms and use different notes, but when we step back and listen to the music, we still want to hear it breathing.

In these final two examples we'll develop some ideas over a Dm7 to Ebm7 groove, like the chord changes to Miles Davis' *So What* or John Coltrane's *Impressions.*

When you come to practice on your own to a metronome or drum groove, it might be useful to refer to this summary of the bass player's tools that are at our disposal:

- Start by picking notes that are happening in the music (i.e., strong chord tones). The root and 5th are the most stable notes, but then we can add the b3 and b7

- Next, look to add more color by using chromatic approach notes to lead into or out of chord tones

- To begin to create more motif-like ideas, the pentatonic and blues scales are a great place to start because they offer different note choices, yet are very stable and won't stray too far from the harmony

- To go further, you can use techniques like applying more interesting scale choices, but to do this you'll have to use your ears and be mindful of the context you're playing in. Plus, what you play must lead somewhere, i.e., back into the harmony

Here's the first variation on the changes. Creating a groove isn't just about the notes we choose and the rhythms we play, it's also about the *space between* the notes. It's about what we choose *not* to play, which allows the other instruments to be highlighted and creates that magical interaction between the band.

Listen to any legendary bassist, such as Bootsie Collins, James Jamerson, Ron Carter, Sting, Ray Brown or Paul Chambers, and you'll notice how they use space. Between them they have created some amazing, memorable basslines, but they wouldn't have been great if they had played all the time, because there wouldn't have been room for anyone else.

So, in this example we are thinking about our phrasing and leaving space for the music to breathe. If we were playing this with other musicians, it would open up space for them to be clearly heard and create the musical interaction we're after.

When we play along to a metronome, we're just responding to that 1/4 note pulse and we'll be inclined to play more notes. This is fine when we're practicing and working on our groove and time, but when we play with a drummer, there will be other "notes" to be mindful of as the drummer uses the kick, snare and hi-hats, so we need to respond accordingly.

Example 1g is played to a drum groove. Listen to how I've adapted my bass part to fit with the drums. There's no point in playing something rhythmically that the drummer is already playing (on the hi-hats, for instance). We need to listen to the drummer and create a part that complements what they are playing, while taking care of bottom end business.

Example 1g

Remember that the drums and bass are the heart and lungs of the band, and while the drums provide the rhythmic pulse of the music, the bass helps it breathe and guides it harmonically. Together, the bass and drums are a heart and lung machine!

This means that the drummer and bassist are dependent on each other. When there is no heartbeat, we can't breathe; and if there is no oxygen, there won't be a heartbeat. It's a symbiotic relationship and all great rhythm sections have figured out how to function together in this way.

With this in mind, I want to dispel a common myth amongst bass players, which is that the bass must *always* match the pattern of the kick drum. I hear this said a lot, but I beg to differ. Your breath doesn't match your heartbeat, right? The two are related, but your heart doesn't beat at the same frequency as your breath.

In the same way, the drums and bass just need to work together with the aim of complementing one another. We may sometimes play on the same beats and sometimes not, but the most important thing is that we work as a single unit.

Here is a different take on the progression. In the previous example, we only had to be aware of what the drums were playing and work on complementing them by sometimes playing in unison and sometimes playing opposing parts. This time we add a guitar, so we have another rhythmic element in the music to be aware of.

Example 1h

As you will have heard, there was a lot more going on in this example and I played more simply to allow the music to breathe.

When another band member is playing a specific part, we don't want to step on their toes and play something that obscures it – we want to support and complement them.

When playing in this kind of context, I'm often thinking about signaling where the 1 is. When the music is busy, I want to make it even clearer where beat 1 is, so that everyone, including the audience, knows exactly where the music is going.

However, if the other musicians make space, we shouldn't be afraid to fill it. Don't turn on your autopilot – keep listening to what your bandmates are doing. This is what makes music fun, unpredictable and magical – when we're all listening intently and wondering who's going to take the lead and show us where we're going next!

That's when things really start to groove.

Chapter Two – Rhythmic and Harmonic Development

In this chapter we're going to take the modal progression we used at the end of the previous chapter and look at lots of different ways to vary the bassline. We'll again look at things from the two main points of view: *rhythm* and *harmony*.

In other words, we'll consider the phrasing we use to create grooves and the note choices we decide on to influence the harmony. Combined, these musical decisions can exert a huge bearing on the feel and mood of any tune we play.

As always, our aim is to play an interesting bassline that guides the direction of the music, while not losing sight of the groove – which we must keep anchored down for our bandmates. This is one of the reasons why I base so much of my musical vocabulary around *motifs*. They are the ideal tool to achieve both aims.

Simply put, a motif is a short musical idea that is repeated. Once stated, the motif can be developed in many ways, and can be rhythmic or harmonic, or both.

For example, Wagner's *Flight of the Valkyries* uses a five-note rhythmic motif (i.e., the rhythm remains the same, but the notes change), whereas the dramatic four-note motif that opens Beethoven's *Fifth Symphony* is an example of a harmonic motif, where the notes are repeated but developed rhythmically.

In modern jazz, we can take more liberties than a classical composer. The motif is a great tool for the jazz bassist because it can help us develop a *theme* for our bassline and solo improvisations. It can give us a strong, core idea that will help everything to hang together.

At its heart, the motif is a storytelling device and using it will result in much more melodic, purposeful bass vocabulary.

In the examples that follow, we'll begin by playing a motif-led bassline that will blossom into a full-blown motif-based solo. We're playing over a modal harmony similar to that used by Miles Davis for *So What*, cycling half step movements between Dm7 and Ebm7.

In Example 2a we set the mood for the piece by beginning with a rhythmic motif.

We also need to think about the note choices being used. We're playing over a Dm7 chord, which comprises the notes D (root), F (b3), A (5th) and C (b7). In this motif the root and the b7 are the most prominent notes and the 5th (by way of the open A string) is used as a kind of pedal tone. The b3 (F) makes an appearance too, just briefly in bar four.

Rhythmically, there are two things to note here.

First, we hit the D root note on beat 1 of bar one, but in every subsequent bar we anticipate the root and slide into it, rather than hitting it dead on the beat. This is a key element in creating the groove. Listen to the audio to get the exact articulation used.

Second, the rhythmic hook of the motif is a 1/4 note, followed by a staccato 1/8th note, two quick 1/16th notes, and another staccato 1/8th note. You'll hear that these rhythmic combinations have a major impact on the groove and feel.

Example 2a

Example 2b is the first variation on this motif. It uses the same basic rhythmic framework laid down in the previous example, but varies it slightly and alters the notes choices.

In bar one, we swop the b7 (C) for the b3 (F) and turn this into a bluesy phrase at the beginning of bar two. For the rest of this bar and bar three, we return to the original note choices of the motif.

In Example 2c we'll be modulating up a half step to play over an Ebm7 chord, so the phrase in bar four of Example 2b is played to transition into the new tonal center.

Example 2b

Now we have four bars of playing over Ebm7 (Eb, Gb, Bb, Db). In bar one, we stay with the essence of the rhythmic motif and use root, b3 and b7 chord tones.

You'll notice that in laying down the basic harmony, the root, b3 and b7 tones are often featured. That's because they are the most important notes (known as *shell voicings* or *guide tones*) in defining the sound of the chord.

The root defines the tonal center, the 3rd tells us whether the chord is major or minor and, taking that information into account, the 7th tells us whether we're dealing with a minor 7, major 7 or dominant 7 chord. Guide tones are so useful because we could even leave out the root note and still get the essence of the harmony.

Example 2c

Next, we modulate back to the tonal center of D Minor. In bar one we use every note of the Dm7 chord, then add some embellishment in the latter half of bar two with an ascending run.

Since our tonal center is D Minor, we could build melodic motifs using a scale that perfectly fits the harmony, such as D Minor Pentatonic (D, F, G, A, C). That scale contains every chord tone of Dm7 and adds a G note (the 4th/11th interval). Or we can draw from other minor scales to access more colorful note choices.

There are two ideas used in the seven-note run in the latter half of bar two. The first four notes come from the D Blues scale. This has the same five notes as the D Minor Pentatonic scale but adds an Ab note – the bluesy b5 tone.

The remaining three notes of the run use a chromatic passing note placed between two chord tones. In other words, we play a C note (b7 of Dm7), then a Db note (a note that does not belong to the D Minor parent key), then the D root note.

Example 2d

In Example 2e we return to restate the main motif, with some variation in bar two. We can move a long way from our original idea and explore different melodic avenues, but when we return to the motif where we began, it will give a sense of continuity to our basslines and solos.

At the end of bar three/beginning of bar four, sliding into notes from below gives this embellishment a bluesy feel and allows us to float over the pulse of the music.

Example 2e

In bar two of this example manipulating the motif rhythmically adds a funky feel. The syncopated phrase begins on beat 2& of the bar with a ghost note. Check out the audio to get the exact timing and feel. Staccato 1/8th notes help to accentuate the groove.

In bar four we play a blues-based lick as an embellishment that fills the whole bar, using the notes of D Minor Pentatonic. The deeper we get into the tune, the more we can embellish the motif and begin to push its boundaries while retaining the feel of the groove.

Example 2f

Here is a longer example that spans the modulation to Ebm7 and back to Dm7.

In bars 1-4 we stick to the main motif and, in bar four use a chromatic approach note idea to target the D root note that falls on beat 1 of bar five. The idea here is to play two passing notes below the root, then the root itself.

In bar eight, using a D Minor Pentatonic lick we signal that this part of the tune is coming to an end and something different is about to happen.

In the following examples, we'll explore some soloing ideas over the progression, but rather than just slip into the solo, it's good to mark this event in the music in a clear way so that everyone (including the audience) can easily follow.

Example 2g

Now it's time to take a bass solo. Through the examples that follow you'll see that the solo is built gradually on a simple rhythmic motif, which then becomes the theme of the solo.

Example 2h states the motif in bars 1-2.

The idea is to focus on just one note, played with a highly syncopated groove. It's played mostly with punchy 1/16th notes and 1/16th note rests, to break up the phrasing. Each expression of the phrase ends with a staccato 1/8th note before it begins again. I chose the b7 (C) of the Dm7 chord as the featured note.

In terms of varying this idea, we can start the motif on a different beat, as in bar one here, where we begin on beat 2. Displacing a phrase to begin in a different place in the bar is an easy way to create rhythmic interest. Plus, we can vary which 1/16th notes we choose to play and to rest, which will alter the syncopation of the phrase.

We can also replace rests with ghost notes. A one-note motif sounds deceptively simple, but in fact there's a lot we can do with one note!

Listen to the audio to nail the articulation of the D Blues scale lick in bar four.

Example 2h

This next idea starts simple and grows in complexity, but it's all still rooted in the original motif. We can jump to a completely new zone of the fretboard without it feeling disconnected from the previous ideas we've played because we're still using the same theme.

We're also changing the harmony of the motif, now focusing on the b3 (F) of Dm7. In bar two we embellish the motif with a quick D Blues lick, then play a more complex bluesy phrase in bars 3-4.

In bar three, the lick is rooted in D Minor Pentatonic and uses two rakes across the muted strings to create a fluid phrase. Begin with your hand in 10th position on the fretboard, so that your first finger plays the notes on the 10th fret while your third finger takes care of the notes at the 12th. Leave your hand in position throughout this bar.

After playing the first phrase, fret the A string, 12th fret with your third finger and allow your first finger to rest lightly on the D and G strings at the 10th fret. Then pluck across the muted top strings to land on the A string note.

You'll need to briefly move out of position to play the blues lick in the second half of bar four.

Example 2i

An important skill for any bass player to develop is to know not only what notes make up a particular chord, but where they are located across the fretboard.

It's all too easy to get stuck in our comfort zones on the fretboard and go to our default, safe places, but developing a visual map of a chord across the neck will lead to a greater degree of harmonic and melodic freedom.

In the previous example, the featured note was an F (b3 of Dm7), and moving up a half step to Gb gets us to the b3 of Ebm7 to mark the change of harmony.

Without a strong sense of visualization, we'd probably be tempted to focus only on root notes to change chord. Try using some fretboard mapping software online during your practice times and work with one chord at a time, playing the notes everywhere on the neck.

These bars feature more "outside" sounding melodic ideas than we've used previously. The freedom of the one-chord vamp allows us to play extended or altered notes over the chord. As long as we eventually resolve those tensions to a stable chord tone, we'll still be able to ground the harmony.

The lick in bar two is played in 11th position. It's easy to visualize the notes of an Ebm7 arpeggio here, with the root note on the E string, but we can work around those notes to find tensions that will make the harmony more colorful.

This line contains the b3, 5th and b7 of Ebm7, but also adds the tense sounding #9, #11 and major 7 tones. On balance, chord tones outweigh the altered tones, but it gives the line an element of harmonic surprise.

Check out the octave idea in bar three. Here the note choices move from the Eb root to the b3 (Gb), an F note (the 9th), and finally a D (the tense-sounding major 7).

In bar four we move back to a more inside-sounding Eb Minor Pentatonic phrase. Look out for the fast 1/16th note ghosted triplet mid-bar. Mute the strings and rake across them as before.

Example 2j

As we get deeper into the solo, we can afford to become more adventurous with our ideas. This line begins with a D Minor Pentatonic riff in bar one that ends on the D root note on the first beat of bar two. Then we begin an ascending passage of notes. Let's break this idea down, starting from the open A string note.

The twelve-note run in bar two uses the notes of the D Natural Minor scale and includes one chromatic passing note (a B note that targets the C chord tone just before the end of the bar).

At the beginning of bar three, another passing note (Gb) is used to connect F and G scale tones. The eight-note phrase that follows uses the notes of the D Dorian scale (D, E, F, G, A, B, C).

D Dorian is identical to D Natural Minor, apart from its sixth degree. D Dorian has a major 6th (B) compared to the b6 (Bb) of the natural minor scale. Playing a B note over a D minor chord implies the sound of Dm6, which brings a different color to the harmony.

The final three notes of bar three (and the first note of bar four that completes the phrase) are tension notes, respectively the major 7, 9th, #9 and #11. In jazz improvisation, tension notes are most often played on up-beats, while strong chord tones are played on down-beats, but if you want to grab people's attention, playing an outside tension right on beat 1 of a bar will do it.

Example 2k

The next example over Dm7 begins with a question and answer phrase.

Used extensively in the blues, the idea is to make a melodic statement (the question) and reply to it (the answer) using similar phrasing, or similar notes played in a different register. Here, the line on the G string in bar one is answered by the line on the A string in bar two.

I chose a different minor scale for the opening two-bar lick to bring another color to the solo. Here, the notes come from the D Harmonic Minor scale.

It's identical to the D Natural Minor scale, except that it has a major 7 (C#) compared to the b7 (C) of the natural minor. Over the D Minor harmony, the C# note implies the sound of a Dm(Maj)7 chord.

What's so useful about this scale is that the C# strongly wants to resolve to the D root note, which makes it a simple but effective tool for creating and resolving tension.

In bars 3-4 we return to the D Dorian scale for our note choices. This ascending line uses every open string as it moves across and up the fretboard, and this device can be tricky to execute cleanly.

On the audio, I'm playing on upright bass, but you can play this line on a standard electric bass too. Apply some careful fretting hand choking of the notes to control how much the open strings ring out.

Example 2l

The next four-bar section begins with an idea built around the D Dorian scale. After a nod to Miles in bar one, we play an ascending line on the G string that climbs chromatically. This note sequence begins and ends on a Dm7 chord tone, with passing notes in between.

In bar three we're borrowing a phrase from Latin Jazz, based around the notes of another minor scale: D Melodic Minor. Using the D Natural Minor scale as our benchmark, the melodic minor scale raises both the 6th and 7th degrees. D Melodic Minor has the notes D, E, F, G, A, B, C#.

In bar four, the opening five-note phrase returns to the natural minor scale, followed by a descending chromatic pattern, and the line ends on the 5th (A) of Dm7.

Example 2m

As we modulate up a half step to Ebm7 we mark the change with another single-note motif.

For this line, I used the Eb Harmonic Minor scale throughout. It comprises the notes Eb, F, Gb, Ab, Bb, Cb, D. The D tension note serves the same purpose as before and wants to resolve to the Eb root note. We play the D note several times during this line and it really brings out the exotic sound of the scale.

Example 2n

In Example 2o we mark the modulation back to Dm7 with a D root note in bar one, but we play the first few notes on the off beats to keep things rhythmically interesting.

In bar three, the articulation in this phrase is achieved by sliding into the notes on the G string from a whole step below, to give it a fluid feel.

The opening phrase is repeated immediately, which means it begins again on beat 3 of the bar. On the repeat, the lick turns into a fast descending run of 1/16th note triplets. It's easier to hear how this sounds than read it, so take a listen to the audio to capture the exact phrasing and articulation.

Example 2o

After exploring some different melodic and harmonic avenues, Example 2p refers back to the motif played in Example 2i. The line ascends the G string, then begins to descend in bar three using the D Dorian scale. We end with a bluesy pentatonic lick in bar four.

Example 2p

The opening lick of Example 2q uses an idea reminiscent of Stevie Wonder's *I Wish* but adds a Db passing note to this D Dorian line to target the D root note at the beginning of bar two.

Bar two has one of the most challenging lines of the solo so far, with an ascending run of 1/16th note triplets.

To learn this line, ignore the first open A string to begin with, and just focus on the triplet patterns. First of all, just learn the shape of the line, regardless of the rhythm, and work out the most economical way of fingering it. Then, begin to play the triplet rhythms.

The line is played legato, so you'll pluck the first note in each group of three, then hammer on to the other notes. The technique of playing legato could occupy a chapter all of its own, but the main tip I'll pass on is to aim for consistency of volume. Don't pick the first note so hard that it's much louder than the hammered notes. Also keep an eye on your timing when playing legato as it's easy for things to become loose.

Example 2q

Now we modulate to Ebm7 one last time. In bar one, the ascending run uses the notes of Eb Natural Minor to move up the G string into the higher zone of the fretboard. In bar two, we hit a B tension note on beat 1, which makes a #5 sound over Ebm7, then descend to a Gb chord tone (the b3). The same phrasing idea is repeated higher up the neck, beginning on Db (b7) and ending on the high Eb root.

At the beginning of bar three, I included a *side-stepping* idea for the first four notes.

This is the concept of playing a phrase a half step above or below where we would normally play it. In this example, it's a shift of a half step above.

If we moved the notes down a half step, they would all be Eb Natural Minor scale notes. Shifting above or below the tonal center immediately creates a set of tension notes, which we can then resolve by moving back inside.

Surprisingly, when shifting an "inside" sounding phrase to an "outside" position, the result is usually not a set of completely chromatic notes as one might expect. Often, the movement will yield extended or altered notes to the underlying chord. In this case, the notes D, C, A, played over an Ebm7 chord are the major 7, 13th and #11.

The phrase that follows the side-stepping movement takes us back inside the harmony with the notes of the Eb Natural Minor scale. The phrasing is tricky in bar three, so listen to the audio to capture the right feel and timing.

Example 2r

To end the solo, we get back into the same zone of the fretboard where we began but continue the idea of applying fluid articulation to our phrases with legato slides into the notes. In bar four, we return to the staccato phrasing of the original motif to bring the solo to an end. From here we could segue back into the original bassline groove, while someone else takes a solo.

Example 2s

In the next chapter we'll continue to explore how we can use motifs to craft creative basslines – this time over more involved chord changes.

Chapter Three – Developing Motifs Over Chord Changes

In the previous chapter, we began to look in depth at how we can develop our basslines rhythmically and harmonically. We did so over a simple, modal minor chord vamp, which shifted up and down a half step.

Playing over static chord vamps is a big part of contemporary jazz and fusion, because it gives the soloist a blank sheet of paper to work with and lots of freedom for expression. However, we also need to develop the skill of playing over chord changes, and that's what we'll explore in this chapter.

By now you now that I *think* in motifs, whether I'm holding down the bottom end bassline or soloing. To me, placing motival ideas at the heart of my approach means that I'm always going to play something melodic, and which has musical meaning – they're never just random notes. Creating a theme for your improvisation is the best way to engage an audience in what you're playing and tell a story with your melodies.

Many great jazz musicians have taken a "cellular" approach to improvisation – John Coltrane and Michael Brecker being among the foremost exponents – where melodic ideas are broken down and organized into smaller, more manageable structures.

To me, using motifs is similar to the Coltrane approach of creating then adapting small musical cells. Either way, you are using simple building blocks as the foundation for what you play.

In this chapter, we'll take one of the most frequently used progressions in jazz, then add some common twists to it. Using this structure, we'll look at how to compose motival ideas that navigate the chord changes, while still having something musically interesting to say.

We'll start with the Major ii – V – I sequence. I'm sure you're already familiar with the Roman numeral naming convention for the chords in a key, so I won't explain that here. In the key of C Major, chord ii is Dm7, chord V is G7, and chord I is Cmaj7.

For this chapter, I played three improvised solos. We're going to take four-bar ideas from the first two solos and analyze the ideas being played. Then we'll break down the third solo too, in order to work towards playing it as a single performance piece.

Major ii – V – I lines

In Example 3a we play the motif or cellular idea that will serve as the foundation for every idea that follows.

The motif uses only scale tones from the C Major scale. There are no chromatic approach notes from outside the key, so the motif can fit over every chord in the ii – V – I sequence. The notes will have a slightly different effect over each chord.

Coltrane used four-note cells as the focus of his playing, and this idea can also be described as a cell, because we're using just the notes D, G, A and B to begin with.

In bar one, over the Dm7 chord (D, F, A, C), the notes of the cell represent the stable root (D) and 5th (A) notes, plus the extended 11th (G) and 13th (B) notes.

The cell is repeated note-for-note over G7 (G, B, D, F). You can see that the cell contains three of its four chord tones and the A note now becomes the 9th over G7.

Bar three repeats most of the cell, but here we begin to embellish it. In bars 1-2, a D note at the 12th ended each bar, and in bar three we descend scale-wise to that note. The phrase ends in bar four with two Cmaj7 chord tones.

Example 3a

Example 3b is the first development of our motif. Here, we keep the phrasing very similar to keep the rhythm of the motif going, but play different notes over the chords, still using just C Major scale notes.

In this line, the "gravity notes" (the ones that stand out, or carry the most weight) are the fifth note in each bar, and they stand out because they are followed by an 1/8th note rest.

In other words, for each chord we play a four-note cell, followed by an additional note, and that fifth note gives us the opportunity to highlight a particular chord tone.

In bar one, it's the F note that falls on beat 3, the b3 of Dm7.

In bar two, it's the A on beat "3&", which is the 9th of G7. (We displaced that note onto an off-beat here, to create some rhythmic surprise).

In bar three, the gravity note is the G on beat 3, the 3rd of Cmaj7.

Example 3b

The next example keeps the motif rhythm in bars 1-2, and the first half of bar three, but changes the notes of the melodic cell again. In bar one, the cell notes over Dm7 are C, A, F, D, which is an inverted Dm7 arpeggio beginning on the b7.

In bars 2-3, the cell changes to B, G, E, C, using the same notes for both G7 and Cmaj7. Over G7, these notes represent the 3rd, root, 13th and 11th respectively. When played over Cmaj7 they represent an inverted Cmaj7 arpeggio.

Example 3c

For the next line, we begin by restating the original motif in bar one. This is a reminder for the listener of the cellular idea that we began with, because in bar two we'll play something more harmonically interesting over the dominant V chord.

Returning to a motif and repeating it note for note is a great way to build a sense of continuity into your solo. It emphasizes the idea that your solo has a theme and is telling a story.

Bar two contains the first chromatic note we've used so far. The four-note cell on which the phrase is based uses the notes Ab E B D – the b9, 13th, 3rd and 5th of the G7 chord. Beginning the phrase on the b9 to create a G7alt sound adds some harmonic interest to the line.

Example 3d

In jazz improvisation, it's often said that one idea informs the next. We can look at an idea in isolation and wonder how the improviser arrived there but, often, improvised lines can only be explained by what went before and this is especially true of motif-based playing.

For example, in bar one of the next idea, the first line is a development of the motif we played in bar one of Example 3b, which itself was a development of the motif in Example 3a!

The rest of the line could also be seen as a development of Example 3b, because we're working in the same zone of the neck, though we're breaking up the phrasing and using more notes.

In bar two, we outline a G7b9 chord by playing only the b9 and the 3rd, with doubled notes. Played over the underlying harmony on the track, this is actually all we need to create that sound.

Over the Cmaj7 chord, we are using the notes of Cmaj7 (C, E, G, B) and C6 (C, E, G, A) arpeggios to spell out the harmony. Rhythmically, this line is more complex, mixing triplets of different note lengths, so be sure to check out the audio track to capture the timing and feel.

Example 3e

Now we've broken free of the rhythm of the original motif and can explore other ideas. This line is composed mostly of 1/8th notes but played with a swinging, underlying 1/8th note triplet feel.

The idea here is to play a phrase that rises and falls over the changes. The ascending line in bar one targets an A note to end on, so that the line in bar two can move down a half step to begin on Ab (b9) before descending. Using half step movements to outline chord changes always sounds great.

Example 3f

To end this first short solo, here is a descending line that moves through the chord changes using repeated notes for emphasis.

Example 3g

ii – V Motifs with Minor 3rd Modulation

For the next set of examples we're going to use an idea that crops up frequently in modern jazz harmony: moving chords or melodic phrases in minor 3rds. If you're unfamiliar with this concept, once you've played through the following examples, you'll begin to hear this idea everywhere.

The essence of the concept is to add richness to the harmony but also tension, by creating a delayed resolution. We expect the ii – V movement (Dm7 to G7) to resolve to the I chord (Cmaj7), but instead it shifts up a minor 3rd (three frets) and we have a ii – V in another key (Eb Major).

Often, the new V chord (Bb7 in this case) will resolve to the original I chord (Cmaj7), which we can achieve with a whole step movement, but equally it is often left unresolved to create a more open sound and the resolution is delayed for longer.

Movements in minor 3rd leaps are symmetrical, which means that if we keep doing it, we'll end up back where we started. E.g., Dm7 to Fm7 (minor 3rd), Fm7 to Abm7 (minor 3rd), Abm7 to Bm7 (minor 3rd), Bm7 to Dm7 (minor 3rd).

This idea is typically used two ways in jazz. First, the minor 3rd shift can be written into the chord changes, so that the whole band play it – which is the way we are using it here.

Second, it's worth noting that a soloist can use minor 3rd shifting ideas in their melodies, even if those chords are *not* written in the harmony. This is the idea of *implied changes*. In other words, suggesting chord changes that are not written to add more interesting extended or altered notes, but playing those notes over the original, less exciting, chords.

This is an idea that goes back to Charlie Parker and the birth of bebop. You only have to compare his tunes *Now's the Time* (a straight three-chord blues in F) to *Blues for Alice* (another blues in F, but including all of the chord changes and substitution ideas that were in Parker's head, written down) to grasp the idea.

We'll begin our exploration of this shifting harmony by playing the motif we started with in Example 3a. Now, our challenge is to develop this motif while moving between two key centers.

When changing to a new key center, it's helpful to identify a pivot note (a note shared by the two chords you're playing over) that will help you move seamlessly between the two tonalities.

In bar three, we start the line over Fm11 with a G note on the top string. It's the root note of the G13 from the previous bar and the 9th of Fm11 (F Ab C Eb G Bb) and it helps to make the transition smoother.

Example 3h

In the next example we repeat the motif and move it onto the D string as we've done before. This gradually ascending line keeps the rhythm of the motif going throughout. In bar two, we anticipate the change of key center by playing a Bb note early. This is the 11th of Fm11 and the root of Bb13, and so hints at the new ii – V movement.

Example 3i

Next, a departure from the motif to play a more free-flowing line as the solo develops. Remember, this is really one long solo that we're breaking into smaller parts to analyze, so the two notes in the pickup bar are Bb13 chord tones (although they look like chromatic approach notes here).

In bar one, I'm thinking about the chord tones of a Dm11 chord. In this line, the notes falling on the downbeats are mostly extended tones, beginning with the 11th (G) on beat 1. Emphasizing these chord extensions gives the line a much more open sound. Add plenty of expressive articulation to the ascending phrase in bar four!

Example 3j

The straight 1/8th note rhythm of this next example helps to tie together the two key centers, while giving the line some momentum. At the end of bar two/beginning of bar three, the half step movement from A (9th of G7) to Ab (b3 of Fm11) is effective in signaling the change of tonal center.

Example 3k

The next line is designed to bring some rhythmic surprise and variety to break up the solo. The idea of using low notes as pedal tones is carried through all four bars and becomes a type of new motif.

Example 3l

Example 3m is a more challenging descending/ascending line for you to try. The challenge is to execute it cleanly and perfectly in time, while using a wide range of your instrument.

In bar one, we're hitting Dm9 chord tones on the first note of each group of three. You may notice a chromatic passing note thrown in there too. Extended notes are placed on the downbeats for the G13 chord.

In jazz, the ii and V chords make a similar sound, and jazz musicians will often focus on just one of the chords (often the V) over the whole cadence. Bars 3-4 are an example of this approach. Rather than picking out Fm11 chord tones, I'm just thinking "Bb dominant" for both bars. This dictates the fact that the line begins on a Bb note.

If we consider this line from a scalic point of view, it's all the Bb Mixolydian scale (Bb, C, D, Eb, F, G, Ab) ascending stepwise through two octaves.

Example 3m

To end this section, here's a line that uses question and answer phrasing in bars 1-2. After a long delayed resolution, in bar three we omit the minor 3rd shift to Eb Major and resolve to Cma7.

Example 3n

Developing Motifs Over Longer Progressions

In the final set of examples for this chapter we'll break down and analyze a solo played over a more complex chord progression.

Here, we'll again use the minor 3rd shift idea we've been working on, but take it a step further, so that now our progression looks like this:

| Dm9 | G13 | Fm11 | Bb13 |

| Dm9 | Db7#9 | Cmaj9 | Ebmaj9 |

Let's take a moment to consider the new ideas that have been introduced into this longer progression.

In bars 4-5, instead of repeating the Dm9 to G13 ii – V cadence, we play a tritone (b5) substitution and replace G13 with Db7#9 – a common jazz substitution.

The b5 substitution then resolves down a half step to the tonic chord of the progression, Cmaj9. In order to turn around the progression, we might then expect to see an A7 chord, which would resolve nicely to Dm9 to restart the sequence, but instead we have Ebmaj9.

The Ebmaj9 is both a minor 3rd shift, and a b5 substitution. It's a minor 3rd shift from Cmaj9 to Ebmaj9, and Eb major is the tritone of the anticipated A7.

Whenever you set out to tackle a chord progression that has extended chords and a shift in tonal center, my advice is to start by making sure you have a solid grasp of the notes of each chord and can identify where the intervals sit in relation to their root notes.

Take the Cmaj9, for instance. Can you look at your fretboard and instantly drop on the 9th interval of that chord without first playing the root? Can you pick out the b3 and 11th of Fm11?

Often, it's helpful to practice just the two-chord cadences of a progression like this, before trying to connect everything together.

I.e., practice just the Fm11 to Bb13 movement, or just Cmaj9 to Ebmaj9.

Working with two chords, play in free time and find as many ways as you can to move seamlessly from one to the next, covering as much of the neck as possible. This will test how well you know the individual chords, and your ability to visualize them across the fretboard.

Now let's begin to work with the progression in four-bar chunks. You're familiar with playing over this section of the tune, but these lines are busier than the previous ones.

In Example 3o there is a less obvious motif carried through the line, which is to outline each chord on the top string in the same zone of the fretboard. Each occurrence of this serves as a springboard to explore lower notes in the same zone, and this creates a kind of question and answer phrasing.

In bars 3-4 there is an emphasis on notes belonging to the Bb dominant chord, and this whole line can be viewed as the Bb Mixolydian scale.

Example 3o

This line creates a motif-like idea by using similar phrasing for each pair of chords.

First, in bars 1-2, we play a similar rhythmic structure for both chords on the top string. In order to signal the change from Dm9 to Db7#9 we could play the root and drop it a half step. Or we could opt for something more subtle and sophisticated.

How about this b7 to b7 movement? At the beginning of the Dm9 bar we emphasize a C note (b7 of Dm9). At the beginning of the Db7#9 bar we emphasize a B note (b7 of Db7#9). It's a nice half step movement and achieves the same result in a less obvious way.

In bars 3-4, a small cellular idea and a repeating rhythm glue together the change from Cmaj9 to Ebmaj9. On the first beat of each bar, three-note cells are played, constructed from the root, 9th and 3rd. (The latter half of the Cmaj9 bar also uses a cell made from the 9th, 3rd and 11th). The idea of using the root, 3rd, and one extended note gives each chord a much more open sound.

Example 3p

This line features a challenging ascending run over the Dm9 chord.

You'll realize that the majority of the time I'm playing an upright bass, and more often than not my Yamaha SLB300PRO upright electric (though all the lines here can be played on a standard electric 4-string bass). In upright playing, it's normal to utilize the open strings wherever possible, especially in order to change position on the neck.

So, here, playing open strings to launch this ascending run might feel a little unusual for the standard electric bass player. I suggest slowing this right down in order to learn the fingering, then once you've worked out how to navigate the line, practice it to a metronome and gradually bring it up to tempo.

Example 3q

This line also uses a double-motif idea. The Dm9 and Db7#9 chords are both outlined with the same rhythmic cellular idea. The phrase over Dm9 begins on a C (the b7), while the Db7#9 phrase begins on an Ab note. Although Ab is the 5th of the chord, there is another substitution idea behind this line.

We talked earlier about implied changes. If you look at the chord chart for Parker's *Blues for Alice*, you'll notice that whenever he saw a dominant 7 chord, he often imagined that it was a V chord and preceded it with its ii chord.

If we view Db7 as a V chord here, then its corresponding ii chord is Ab minor, and the lick played here outlines an Abm(Maj7) arpeggio over the Db7.

Whenever you see an altered dominant chord such as Db7#9, and can't immediately think what to play over it, playing a pentatonic phrase based on its ii chord (Ab Minor Pentatonic) can be a life saver!

Example 3r

Here's a line that blends 1/8th and 1/16th note phrasing.

The descending run launches from the D root note in the pickup bar, starting its descent from the b7 in bar one.

In bar two we ascend over G7 and add the b9 altered note (Ab) at the end of the bar. The Ab segues nicely into the Fm11 chord in bar three (now functioning as the b3).

For the line in bars 3-4, the notes come from the Bb Mixolydian scale. Note that in the final phrase of bar four, the notes in brackets are ghost notes and don't sound.

Example 3s

In Example 3t, you'll need to execute another fast run that launches from two open strings – upright style. Get your fretting hand in position around 10th position, ready to play the upper register notes.

Work out the most comfortable fingering for this line. Once you're playing on the top string, if you play the 10th, 12th and 14th frets with your first, second and third fingers respectively, you can then jump or slide your first finger in to play the 14th fret again, ready for the slide to the 17th.

From there, you can either slide the first finger again, or slide your second finger and play the D string, 19th fret, with your third finger. The open A string at the end of bar one gives you time to change position again, ready for bar two.

In Example 3r, we looked at a ii chord substitution idea and played an Ab minor type arpeggio over Db7. Expanding on this idea, it's possible to create some great tensions by playing the melodic minor scale based on the ii chord.

So, in bar two, over Db7#9, all the notes come from the Ab Melodic Minor scale (Ab, Bb, Cb, Db, Eb, F, G). The effect of superimposing this scale creates a set of extended chord tones, plus the dissonant sounding #11 altered note.

Example 3t

This last four-bar section of the solo features a fast run down over the Dm9 – G13 change. The same rules as before apply here: work out a comfortable and efficient fingering first, then practice the line slowly to a metronome to master the phrasing. When you're confident, work on increasing the tempo.

The progression finally resolves back to C major in bar three, so we end with a bluesy C major lick.

Example 3u

Now you've practiced all the component parts of the solo, have a listen to the audio for Example 3v and work on playing along with the whole solo. Try and memorize as much as you can, as this is great ear training.

Example 3v – Full Solo

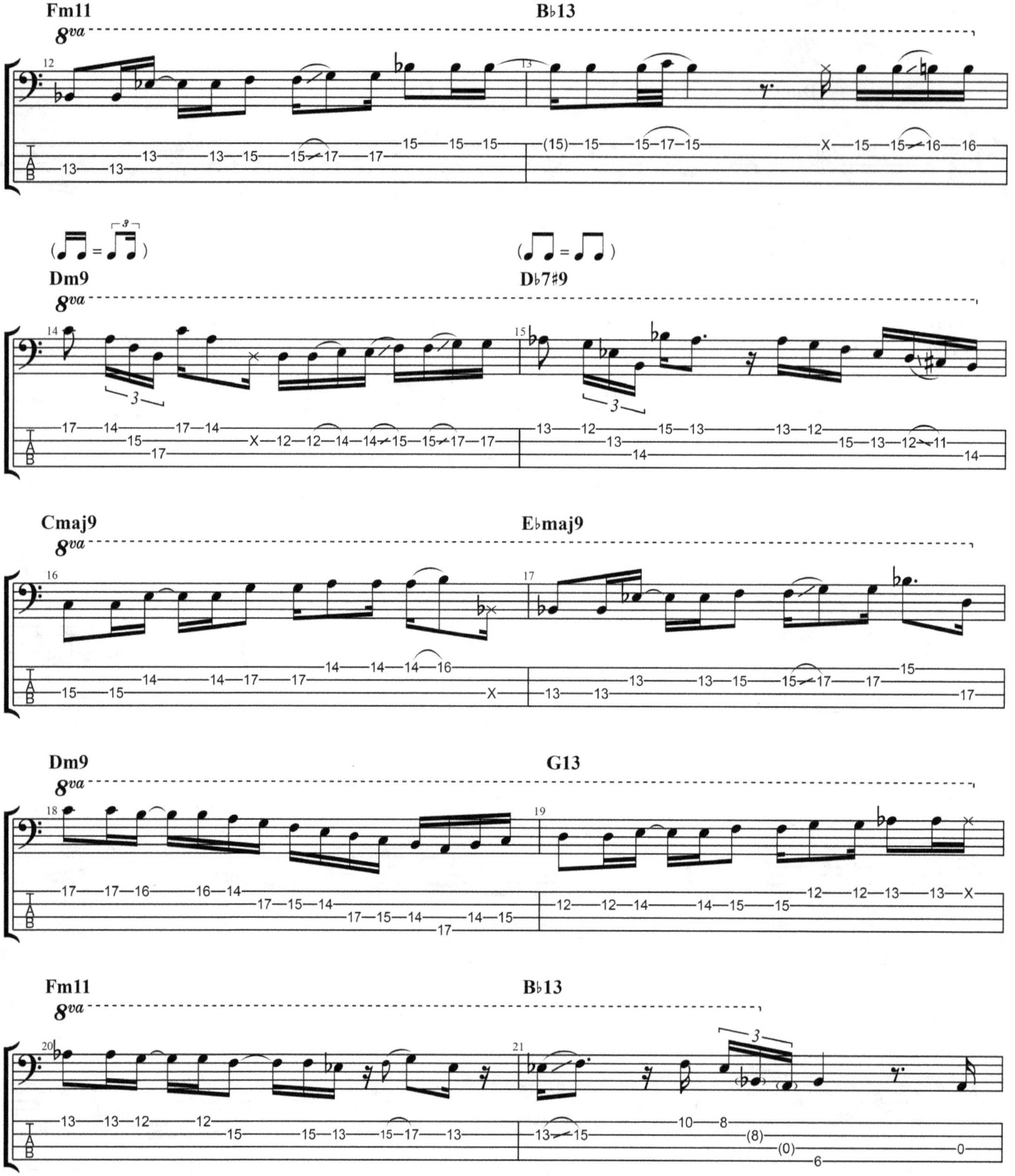
Fm11
B♭13
8va
Dm9
D♭7♯9
8va
Cmaj9
E♭maj9
8va
Dm9
G13
8va
Fm11
B♭13
8va

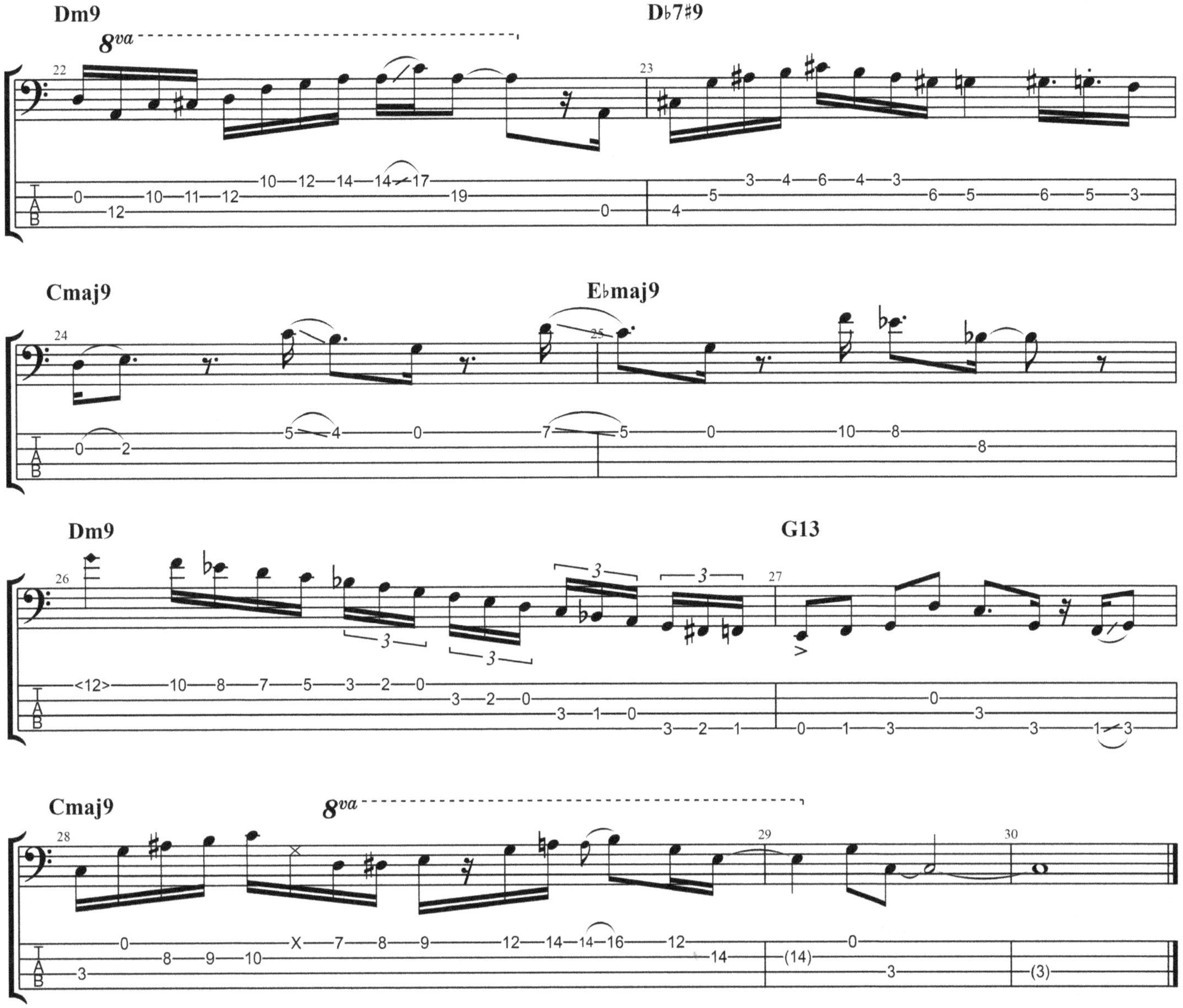
Dm9
8va
D♭7♯9
Cmaj9
E♭maj9
Dm9
G13
Cmaj9
8va

Chapter Four – Creating a Complete Groove & Solo

In this chapter we'll take our motif-based ideas a step further and delve deeper into the skills required to express ourselves in an improvised solo over a tune, adding articulation and advanced phrasing ideas. My aim is to give you an insight into how I think when improvising in a live situation, at the same time as passing on some tools for you to work on this yourself.

We'll play over the chord changes to the popular, funky standard *Sunny*. At the end of this chapter is the complete bass part played on the audio track, but first we'll break down the tune into smaller sections and examine the ideas being used.

To give you a realistic, practical example of how I would approach this tune live, I played a bassline over the chord progression going from simple to more rhythmically complex ideas, then took a solo, then returned to the groove – exactly as I would do in a live performance. The examples that follow demonstrate how to build into, then come down from a solo – a skill that's rarely taught or talked about, but is vital to understand in a live situation.

Bass Part Breakdown

At the beginning of this arrangement of *Sunny*, we play through the chord progression taking a minimalist approach and end with an additional bar of E7#9. This section serves as the introduction.

Here we use a simple rhythmic motif to spell out the chord changes. We hit the root note of the first chord on the beat, then play a short fill, then *push* the root note of the second chord, hitting it just before beat 1 of the next bar.

This pattern continues throughout the introduction. You'll also hear some additional pushed notes mid-bar, as we sometimes play an additional chord tone or the root of a second chord.

Pushing notes helps to create a sense of anticipation and momentum. Think about the timing and play this a few times until you feel you've got it in the pocket.

Example 4a

Now the form of the tune begins proper and we get into the groove. It's a funky tune, so we'll naturally play some syncopated lines to come up with a fitting bassline.

In this example, we keep the idea of hitting the root of the Am7 in bar one on beat 1, and anticipating the Gm9 in bar two. Then we hit the Fmaj7 on the beat, and anticipate the Bm7b5, etc.

To add some syncopation to the groove, I introduced ghost notes into the bassline (marked by an X in the TAB). If you're playing this on a standard electric bass, you can use fretting hand muting to deaden the strings and create the ghost notes. I'm most often playing an electric upright, so I achieve this effect by tapping the strings with my plucking hand. One advantage of doing this on an upright bass is that it also adds a percussive sound, not just a dead note.

You can create some complex rhythmic patterns using this effect. Notice that each time the Am7 is played, the 1/4 note root is followed with a tapped pattern of two 1/8th note triplets followed by a quick 1/16th note.

Simple taps are also highly effective, as in bar three, where the root of the Fmaj7 chord is anticipated by a 1/16th note tapped accent.

Example 4b

We can also create interest by introducing more movement between the chord changes. Compare the first three bars of this example to the relative simplicity of the first three of Example 4a, where we started.

Here, we add 1/8th note accents that "bounce" off the root notes of the chords to create the syncopation we want.

Notice that in bar one, we play the low G note much earlier than before, well ahead of the Gm9 chord change. It works here because G is the b7 of Am7 as well as the root of Gm9 – it's a pivot note.

At the end of bar two, the three-note phrase that leads into the root of Fmaj7 contains notes that don't belong to the Gm9 we're currently playing over. What's happening here? We saw this idea back in Example 3h: the concept of implied chord changes.

Although in this section of the tune the harmony is Gm9 for a whole measure, here we imply the Gm9 to C9 chord change that appears in other parts of the tune. The C and E notes are the root and 3rd of C9, and ending on the 3rd (E) creates a smooth half-step transition up to the root of Fmaj7.

Example 4c

Now we come to the bass solo over the *Sunny* chord changes. During the solo, the keyboard elaborates on the chord changes, adding in some new ideas, which are reflected in the notation below.

In order to start the solo with a strong melodic statement, this four-bar line hints at the melody of the tune without actually playing any part of it.

The trick to achieve this is to use the same phrasing as the melody and, where possible, the same kind of intervallic ideas. Listen to the audio and you'll hear that although the notes are different, the phrases "breathe" at the same points as the melody.

Sunny is in the key of F Major, with a ii – V movement (Bm7b5 – E7) borrowed from A Harmonic Minor. In this example, the F Major scale (F, G, A, Bb, C, D, E) supplies all the melody notes.

Example 4d

The motif we've chosen for this solo thus far is the shape of the original melody. In this example we keep that overall sense of the melody's phrasing but move to the mid-register of the neck for some different note choices.

To add a slightly different flavor to the melody, this time we're using the A Minor scale (A, B, C, D, E, F G) instead of F Major. However, in bar four, because the keyboard plays an E7#9 chord which contains a G#/Ab note, we add that non-scale tone at the start of the final phrase.

There is also more embellishment to the phrases here. Hammer-ons and pull-offs, slides, and even bends on bass can transform a phrase from routine to soulful. But the timing of the phrasing is crucial; aim to sit slightly behind the beat and be aware of not rushing ahead of the time.

Example 4e

In the next part of the solo we introduce a motif based on a rhythmic pattern.

The rhythm is a staccato 1/8th note followed by two 1/16th notes, which creates a bouncing syncopation against the groove. This idea is carried through bars 1-3 as we spell out each chord, then in bar four we break into an ascending run.

The run is played over a Bb13 chord. We've seen this chord played a few times now, and it's a common jazz chord substitution idea used to enrich the harmony.

Before the substitution is applied, the original harmony would read:

Am7 – Gm9 – Fmaj7 – Fm11

We've changed that to:

Am7 – Gm9 – Fmaj7 – Bb13

The substitution works on the basis of shared notes. The two chords have all but one note in common, and playing Bb13 here is similar to playing an Fm11 inversion with its Bb note in the bass. Not only does this enrich the sound of the harmony, it creates a nice half step movement as the bass note moves from Bb to B for the next chord.

Because the addition of this substituted chord momentarily creates a strong Bb tonal center, for soloing we can treat it like a static chord in a modal progression. So, here we are using the Bb Major scale to supply our note choices.

Slow this run down to learn the phrasing. The execution of it is tricky, since it relies on incorporating the open strings, but that is what gives the line its fluid sound.

Example 4f

When taking a solo, we can focus on targeting chord tones in our phrases and keep our lines based around arpeggio ideas (a great way to keep a solo grounded in the harmony) or, alternatively, we can use scale choices to inform our phrases and naturally create some interesting tensions over the chord changes.

Bars 1-2 of this part of the solo use a five-note motif that repeats and is adapted to accommodate the Am7 to Gm7 whole step shift.

In bar one, I opted to use the A Harmonic Minor scale for the note choices. The A Harmonic Minor scale is almost identical to the A Natural Minor scale except it has a major 7th (G#) rather than a b7.

In the latter half of bar one, playing that G# note on beat 3 creates a moment of dissonance or tension, which is resolved by playing a B note (the 9th) for an Am9 sound, followed by the A root note.

The phrase at the end of bar one targets the b3 (Bb) of the Gm9 chord in bar two. For bar two, we revert back to the F Major scale to work around the ii – V cadence that will resolve to Fmaj7.

There is a harmonically/rhythmically complex line for you to work on in bars 3-4. Another strategy we can use to create tension and release in our phrasing is to imply a more complex chord than the one written on the lead sheet. In bar three, I think of the underlying harmony as Fmaj7#11 rather than a straight Fmaj7.

Fmaj7#11 contains the notes F, A, C, E, B and we drop the 7th (C) on beat 1, the root on beat 2, and the #11 (B) on beat 3 in this phrase.

Keeping these clear target notes in view, we can structure the rest of the line so that we hit them on the strong beats. At first listen, the line might sound random, but when you're listening for those target notes, suddenly its structure makes sense.

Rhythmically, this is a straight 1/16th note line. What makes it interesting is that I'm thinking of it as being organized into three-note cells, which you can see most clearly in the TAB.

In bar four, we revert to the idea of playing chord tones, but again I'm thinking of a more colorful chord than the one written.

In jazz, it's common when playing over ii – V cadences to choose just one of the chords to use as your point of reference when soloing. The ii and V chords have a similar sound, so here we can choose to work with a B minor or an E dominant tonality, and play it over both chords. I took the dominant chord route and played an E7b9 (E, G#, B, D, F) arpeggio over the whole bar. This is something I will typically do in a funky song. If I was playing a swinging jazz number that called for a walking bassline, I'd spell out both chords.

Example 4g

Here is an idea that contains two melodic motifs, separated, but connected by a triplet based run.

The first motif occurs in bar one. The idea is to hammer onto a chord tone (G to the A root of Am7) and played a dead note rake down to a lower two-note phrase (A to G).

This idea is repeated in a higher register, this time targeting an extended chord tone (C to D, the latter being the 11th of the chord). Again, the phrase ends by reversing the note order.

This illustrates the importance of articulation in our phrasing. It's possible to create an interesting phrase using just two notes!

The second motif occurs in bar four. It's a simple rhythmic motif that spells out the changes. For the Bm7b5 chord, we emphasize the root note. For the E7, we are highlighting the b9 again.

The line in bars 2-3 which separates these ideas was a spontaneous idea that turned out to be rhythmically complex as I switched up the rhythmic divisions.

While we could break down an idea like this and talk about the rhythms, it's better to listen to the line several times then internalize it in order to learn it. Notation is, after all, just a way of documenting what happened when we played – it's not a perfect way of capturing feel and articulation. For that, we must use our ears.

Example 4h

One of the defining features of the harmony of *Sunny* is that whole step movement from Am7 down to Gm9, so it's always worth highlighting that strong chord change with our melodic lines. On the backing track, the bass is supported by a piano, but it would become even more important to outline that movement if we were playing in a trio setting with drums and guitar, for example.

In this example, the motif is played in the higher register on the top strings. In terms of note choice, we're using A Harmonic Minor over the Am7 chord, and G Harmonic Minor for Gm9.

So far, we've tended to use the F Major scale for the Gm9, but here the harmonic minor introduces a nice tension and means that we can exactly mirror the phrase of bar one, moved down a whole step.

When playing the phrase is bars 3-4, be mindful of your fretting hand control, if you're playing a standard electric bass, so that you accurately reproduce the dead notes. If you're playing an upright, use a combination of fretting muting and tapping the strings with your plucking hand to create a percussive groove.

Example 4i

Example 4j is the climax of the solo and uses a range of articulation techniques to increase the drama of the fast phrasing.

The line is composed mostly of quick 1/16th notes, and the phrasing is punctuated by percussive taps/dead notes, which help to keep things syncopated and grooving.

This approach obviously demands some accurate fretting and muting, so I recommend working through the whole line slowly to begin with, planning an efficient fingering, and initially focusing just on nailing the transitions between played notes and dead notes.

When you're confident with this, add in the articulation. The line begins with a simple hammer-on in bar one, but it's worth practicing the repeating hammer-ons of bar two that are "interrupted" by a dead note.

The ascending line is bar three is the trickiest phrase to play.

After plucking the open A string, play the 5th fret note on the A string with your first finger. Then play the 7th to 8th fret hammer-on on the E string with your second and third fingers. This will leave your first finger free to hop over onto the 5th fret of the D string.

From there, you have fingering options, but I would suggest that you jump your first finger onto the 7th fret of the A string to play the ascending phrase. This will get your fretting hand into position for the next part of the phrase.

From the end of bar three into bar four, keep the legato slides nice and fluid. Notice that as the line comes to an end in bar four, there is a clear signal that the solo has concluded. The very last note (G) doesn't belong to the chord – it's laying down a marker that will resolve to the root of the Am7 chord as the bass drops back into the groove.

Example 4j

It's important to know how to build up to and get into a solo, but also how to find a good exit point. We also need to send a clear signal to our bandmates that we're done.

This is something I'll speak about in more detail in the final chapter, but I felt it was important here to give you a real life example of playing a supporting role, taking a solo, then returning to a supporting role, so that you have a practical example to listen to and copy.

Now that the bass solo has ended, we're back into the groove. After the solo (and let's assume that other band members will also have taken a solo), it's appropriate to ramp up the energy of the accompanying bass part as the tune works towards a conclusion.

Examples 4k to 4o show the supporting bassline for the remainder of the tune. They each contain much more syncopation than at the beginning to keep the energy high and propel the groove forward. If the drums are the heart of the band and the bass is the lungs, here we're giving the lungs a good workout!

These examples also contain some embellishments to the basic bassline and imply some changes to the harmony. Let's take a brief look at each part.

This first example is all about adding more syncopation using a combination of dead notes and tapped notes (if you're not playing an upright bass, they'll all be played as dead notes). The note choices are fairly simple but it's important to nail those accents in between.

Example 4k

This line takes a contrasting approach. Although there are still muted notes to play, this time you'll allow more notes to ring out and play some fills between the chord changes. There's a lot going on here and your goal is to keep things funky and grooving. Listen to the audio to capture the shape of the bassline and work on playing it cleanly.

Example 4l

Here is a variation on the highly syncopated, ghost-note approach, where I've added in some different fills and connecting notes between the chords. In bars 7-8, rather than vamping on Am7 as we've done before, I added an open-sounding chromatic run down to E7. An idea like this is a good "reset" line – like we're ending one chapter and beginning another.

Example 4m

Next, another variation on the progression. Dead notes are used more sparingly and the bassline opens up more, beginning to move away from the funky feel.

Example 4n

In this final example, we've "come down" from the hard grooving feel and the notes ring out more, with limited syncopation. This makes it feel like we're about to bring the tune to a close. Here, we also repeat the motival idea of the chromatic descending line from Am7 down to E7. We're also adding a tag ending (repeating the final four bars) to make it very clear that we're at the end of the tune.

Example 4o

Now, you've worked through every part of the bassline, here is the bass part in full for practicing purposes.

Example 4p – Full Bass Part

B11 E7#9 C6/A B♭6/9
Fmaj7 Bm7♭5 E7 Am7
Gm9 C9 Fmaj7 Bm11 E7#9
Am7 Gm9 Fmaj7
B♭13 B11 E7♭9
Am7 B♭13

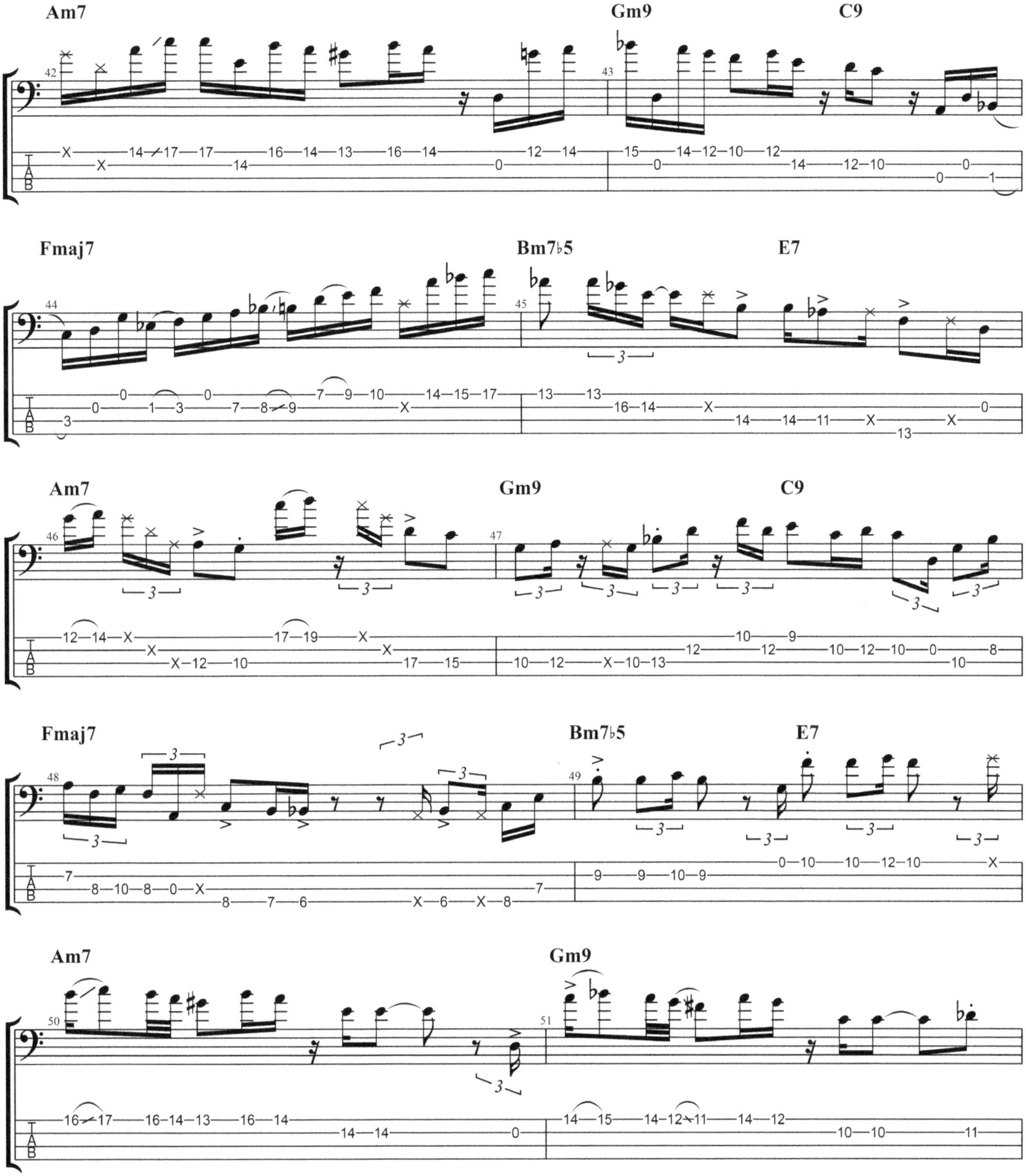
Am7
Gm9
C9
Fmaj7
Bm7♭5
E7
Am7
Gm9
C9
Fmaj7
Bm7♭5
E7
Am7
Gm9

Fmaj7
B♭13
Bm7♭5
E7♯9
Am7
E7♭9
Am7
Gm9
C9
Fmaj7
Bm7♭5
E7
Am7
Gm9
C9
Fmaj7
Bm7♭5
E7
Am7

Gm9
Fmaj7
B♭13
Bm7♭5
E7
Am7
G♭m7♭5
F9
E7
Am7
Gm9
C9
Fmaj7
Bm7♭5
E7
Am7
Gm9
C9
Fmaj7
Bm7♭5
E7
Am7
Gm9
Fmaj7

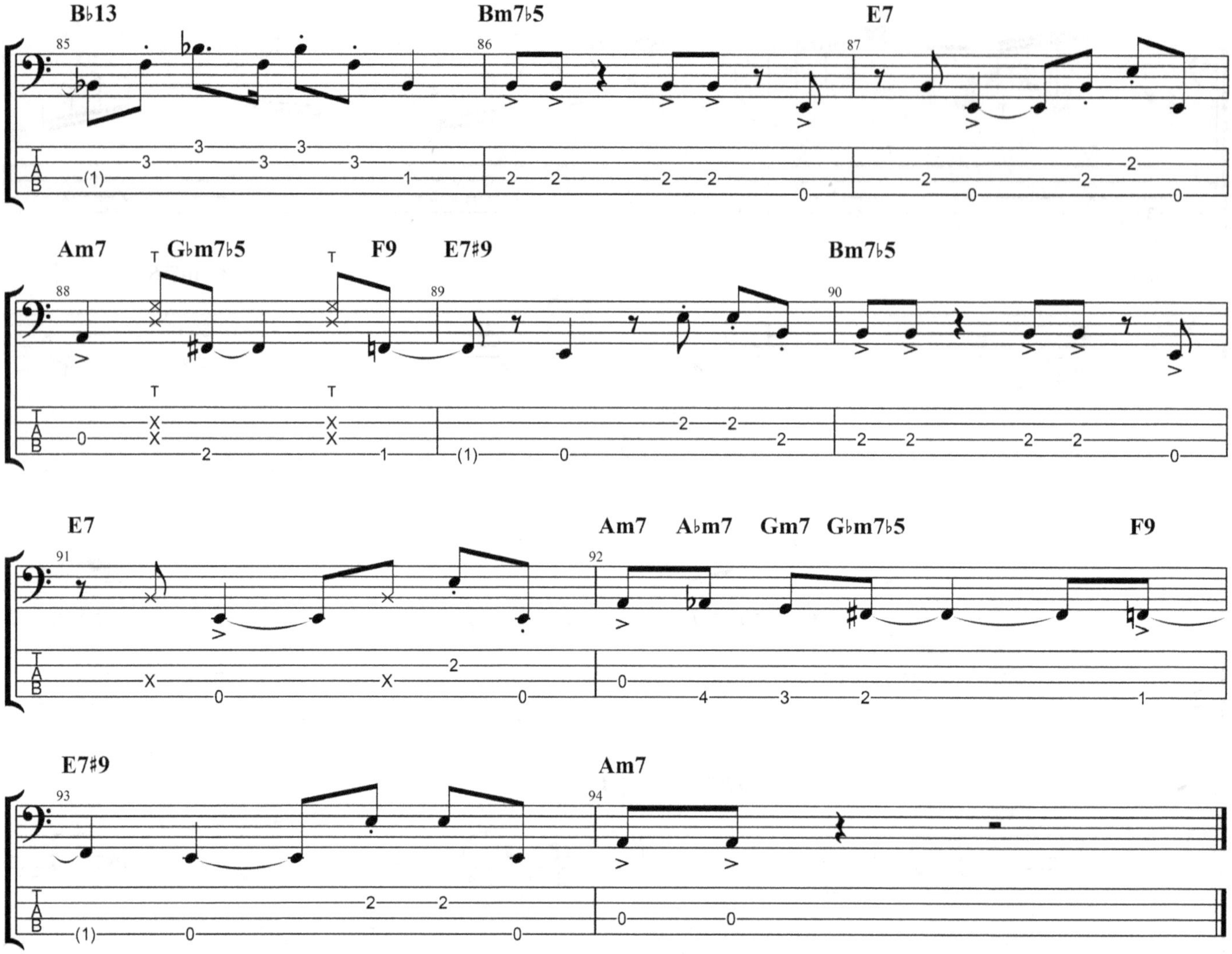
B♭13
Bm7♭5
E7
Am7
G♭m7♭5
F9
E7♯9
Bm7♭5
E7
Am7
A♭m7
Gm7
G♭m7♭5
F9
E7♯9
Am7

Chapter Five – Thinking in Chapters

In this final chapter we're going to repeat the process of laying down a bassline, getting into and out of a solo, then returning to the groove, and I want to pass on some more practical advice about how to do that. I also want to change the way that you think about soloing and give you a new way to frame it in your mind.

Thinking in Chapters

Throughout this book I've spoken about the bass being the "lungs" of the band, and of the responsibility we bass players bear to allow the music to breath. Our main goal is to enable the music to *flow* – and that natural flow should carry over into how we develop our bassline ideas and how we improvise when we take a solo.

One of the questions I'm often asked by students is, "How do you pace a solo?" and "How do you know what the next motif should be?" My answer is to take a step back, and instead of worrying about what motifs you'll use and how you'll develop them, think about creating the overall story of the song with a series of "chapters".

What do I mean by that?

Instead of thinking bar by bar what might work over the changes, think of the different sections of the tune as larger chapters or passages – just like a classical composer might create a movement. Whatever motif you begin with (whether it's a bottom end bassline or a solo), allow that to become the theme of that chapter of the tune. Now you only have one main thing to think about and you can develop your ideas around it.

This means that you can focus on playing a motif and developing it over a longer period, interacting with your other band members as you do so, before moving on to a new idea. That's one chapter in the story of the song. Then you can take the music in a different direction, and begin a new chapter.

Keep this idea in mind as you work your way through this tune and move in and out of the solo.

Starting a Solo

The art of beginning a solo is a skill that shouldn't be overlooked. Before I begin a solo, I want to make it clear to the audience: now it's time for me to play a solo!

Early in my playing career, when it was time for me to solo, it was just like the old cliché: half the audience went to the bar to get a drink and the drummer took the opportunity to adjust the tension on his hi-hat!

So, I wanted to find a way of making people pay attention and "announce" the solo. One way I found was, if I had been playing a busy bassline leading up to the solo, I would just stop playing. Then the audience would think, "What's going on?" It created a "void" which drew people in, then I would begin my solo in a minimalist kind of way.

Try this idea and you'll find it has two benefits: first, it forces the audience to pay attention and engage with what you're doing. Second, your bandmates will react to the silence and pull back, which will give you the peace and space to start your solo by playing what you want. If you begin to solo while everyone else is still grooving, everyone's attention will be divided between what's happening.

Whether you start your solo soft and sparse or loud and funky, taking control of that moment and effectively hitting the "reset" button on the mood of the tune is a great way of setting up your solo.

This is something I developed over time and, frankly, learned the hard way. I got my first gig with Mike Stern when I was 21, and went from playing on the streets and in the small clubs of New York to a 3,000-seat auditorium, and I was very nervous.

It was a trio gig, and after Mike had played an outrageous solo, it was my turn. Safe to say, I didn't create a void! I was afraid to be exposed by the space, so without even taking a beat, I just played everything I could.

It might seem obvious, but if you throw the kitchen sink at the first eight bars of your solo, then you have literally nowhere to go. That's why it's good to take a deep breath and embrace the void. Not only will it optimize your space for soloing, it will open up many more simple ways to start your solo. You don't have to try and match the energy of the other soloists.

Tune Breakdown

In this chapter we'll be grooving and soloing over the chord changes to *Cantaloupe Island*. This is a nice tune to work with because it's modal, using just three chords, and has shifting tonal centers. This gives us a lot of space to express ourselves.

The tune begins by vamping on an Fm7 chord, so here is a laid-back, simple setup bassline for the song.

Example 5a

This example shows the bassline for the first, full chorus of the tune. It follows a simple pattern of playing the root note of the chord on beat 1, followed by the 5th (C) on beat 2& to create a push. Then on beats 4 and 4& we play the b7 (Eb) up to the root. We do this for each chord and the approach fits nicely with the vibe of the tune.

Example 5b

This example keeps the same root + 5th + b7 + root motif going, and now we begin to introduce some variation in the bassline by playing a fill in every fourth bar.

Example 5c

Back in Chapter One we discussed the idea of making the metronome "swing" by controlling note lengths and subtly pushing and pulling the time around that constant pulse. In this example, though the core motif idea remains the same, we're altering the note lengths throughout to bring some variation to the bassline and cause the groove to "breathe" in a different way.

For instance, until this point, we've always played the root on beat 1 as a 1/4 note, and occasionally we'll now change that to a dotted 1/4, increasing its length. This simple alteration changes the phrasing in the bar. We are also adding some fills after those dotted 1/4 notes to gradually increase the amount of movement in the bassline.

Example 5d

This example introduces more variations into the phrasing and begins to move towards the solo section.

You can begin building towards your solo even before you start – either by altering what you play leading into it, thus affecting the vibe and mood of your bassline, or simply by having a first note in mind and smoothly leading into it.

I often have just the first note of my solo in mind, and that will usually be a chord tone. Then I'll consider what route I'm going to take to get to that note before the solo begins. For example, here in bar sixteen I broke out of the bassline pattern, then played two ascending chromatic phrases.

After the final note (F), I then jumped up a minor 3rd interval to play an Ab as the first note of the solo (Example 5f), which is the b3 of the Fm7 chord.

Example 5e

Dm11

Fm7

I then used the Ab note I picked as my opening note as the main feature of a repeating, rhythmic motif to begin the solo. The Ab (b3 of Fm7) bounces off the F root note on the D string, with the latter acting as a kind of pedal tone. Also a feature of this three-note motif is a Bb note. This is an extended chord tone and implies an Fm11 harmony.

Example 5f

Fm7

In the next section of the solo, we continue the idea of moving between two notes on the top string.

We can use this idea to move between chord tones, or cycle between a chord tone and an altered note. In bar one, I wanted to avoid simply playing the root of Db7, so opted for the b7 (B) of the chord, which produces a subtle tension, since it's not the most obvious note choice. The rest of the phrase contains the root and 5th notes, but also the extended intervals of the 9th and 11th.

You can think of this line in terms of picking out certain chord tones, if you know the intervals on your fretboard well, or you can frame it all in a scale choice. The Db Mixolydian scale contains all of the notes apart from the final A note at the 14th fret, which anticipates the idea to come in bar two.

In bar two, I targeted an A note over the Db7 chord and flipped between A and Ab. Ab is the 5th of the chord, which makes A the #5, and the effect is a nice, quick moving inside-outside tension.

Example 5g

One thing I've always tended to do, and which has become more important to me over the years, is that when I solo, I want you to be able to hear which beat I'm aiming for when I play a line.

In other words, I'll improvise a line but know clearly that I'm aiming to start it on beat 4 of a bar, spanning into the next measure, for example. Or, I'll end a phrase on beat 2 or 3, then leave space before beginning a new idea.

Good phrasing is hard to teach and even harder to learn, so the more you practice targeting a specific beat of the bar, the better your phrasing will become.

It's very common for players to begin a phrase well, only for it to tail off and end in a vague manner. To combat this, start by selecting a beat in the bar that you'll end your phrase on, and focus on ending your phrase cleanly on that beat. Then play nothing for a beat before beginning your next phrase.

Over time you'll develop the skill of picking out and targeting specific beats in the bar, moving from 1/4 notes to more complex subdivisions. Not only will your phrasing improve, your sense of time will too.

In this example, my target was beat 3 in bar one. Notice that I emphasize that note, adding some vibrato articulation, then also leave a rest at the beginning of bar two before beginning a new idea. We've ended one chapter, now we're beginning another.

Example 5h

This is one of the busiest lines in the solo as the progression returns to Fm7. The opening line feature a run using a bebop scale and making use of open strings where possible.

Bebop scales are eight-note scales created by adding a passing note to a standard seven-note scale. This idea became prevalent during the bebop era when much of our modern jazz vocabulary was created.

When you want to play long passages of 1/8th or 1/16th notes, using a seven-note scale can create some phrasing challenges, but an eight-note scale is ideal! Plus, the addition of a chromatic passing note adds some tension.

Here, we're using the F Dorian Bebop scale (F, G, Ab, A, Bb, C, D, Eb), which is like a standard F Dorian scale but with a passing A note added between the b3 (Ab) and 4th (Bb). Over the Fm7 harmony, that A note creates a fleeting #9 tension.

In bar two, you can think of this line as a pattern-based idea. We are hitting a mixture of chord tones and extended tensions, but the important note here is the final destination note: the F root on the 10th fret.

As long as we have a target chord tone we're aiming for, which we land on a down-beat, our audience will accept the chromaticism used to get there.

In bars 3-4, you can hear that we're closing this chapter of the solo before moving onto a new one. This F Minor Pentatonic line resets the mood for the next idea.

Example 5i

Now we begin a new chorus of the tune and we can work our way into some different ideas. In bars 1-2, pay attention to the articulation being used, as this kind of idea works best when you're absolutely committed to making it stand out. You'll need to punch out the notes, then slide downwards (as indicated on the TAB) into a string tap or dead note. The taps fall on down-beats.

Example 5j

We move into the higher register for this line played over the Db7 chord. Again, you can think of this line as originating from the Db Mixolydian scale (Db, Eb, F, Gb, Ab, Bb, Cb). Your aim here is to achieve a vocal-like phrasing with the line. When you've learned the line, try singing it at the same time as playing. You'll find that there is a natural, breathing rhythm to the shape of the line.

Example 5k

Now for a fast line over the static Dm11 chord. We're using the D Dorian scale (D, E, F, G, A, B, C) here with the addition of a couple of passing notes. It's not a bebop scale, we're just adding chromatic notes when they conveniently add to the shape of the line.

Notice that we start with a 1/4 note D, which acts as a launch pad for the line as we move into a long 1/16th note passage. This line presents a couple of technical challenges in order to execute it cleanly and achieve a smooth flow to your phrasing.

First, in bar one, you have the hammer-ons followed by string skips to negotiate. The key here is to control unwanted string noise by picking accurately and using some fretting hand muting to lightly damp the un-played strings.

I played this on my upright electric, so I naturally default to using open strings where possible, but if you're using a standard electric bass, you could re-finger it accordingly. However, do include the open G string at the end of bar one, as you'll need this to facilitate a quick change of fretting hand position for bar two.

The challenge of bar two is some fast fretting hand position changes. Start with your first finger on the 7th fret of the D string. After playing those three notes, play the first three notes on the G string with your first, second and third fingers, ending on the 11th fret. For the note at the 12th fret, jump your fretting hand into 12th position and play that note with your first finger. Jump position again to play the note at the 16th fret with your first finger also.

Work on making these transitions sound seamless and keep an ear on your timing. I suggest practicing your fingering for a while at a slower speed to program the movements into muscle memory.

Example 51

This example is the "end of chapter" line that signals the conclusion of the solo. Notice that the pace of the line is slower here, and that we also descend throughout the line. Both these techniques are useful to send a message to your bandmates that you're winding down your solo.

I'm not suggesting this as a blueprint you should use every time, but often when I'm done soloing, I will transition the end of my solo into the lower register and aim to flow seamlessly back into the supporting bassline.

There's nothing worse than ending a solo abruptly then jumping back into the bassline, like those two parts have nothing to do with each other!

I liken it to an Olympic relay race, where you know you're going to pass the baton to your teammate. You want to make that person aware that you're about to pass the baton to them, then make it a smooth transition. You don't want to drop the baton and ruin the whole flow of the race. Similarly, on the bandstand, clear signaling that says, "I'm about to wrap this up, then it's your turn" is really important to keep the flow and momentum.

Example 5m

Now we return to a simple bassline, close to where we began, with some minor embellishments. These bars also lead to a set ending for the tune. The Dm11 chord is extended for an extra two bars, but then we hit the F root note to end.

Example 5n

I trust this has been a useful demonstration of how to build towards a solo, improvise over the changes using motival ideas, and then come down from the solo and smoothly drop back into the groove. I've also endeavored to pass on some tips about stagecraft in the process.

You've practiced every part of the solo, so now try working through the whole thing and slowly chip away at it during your practice sessions. Try to memorize as much as you can, so that you become less reliant on reading the notation/TAB and rely more on your ears.

Also make sure you just have some fun jamming over the backing track!

Example 5o – Full Solo

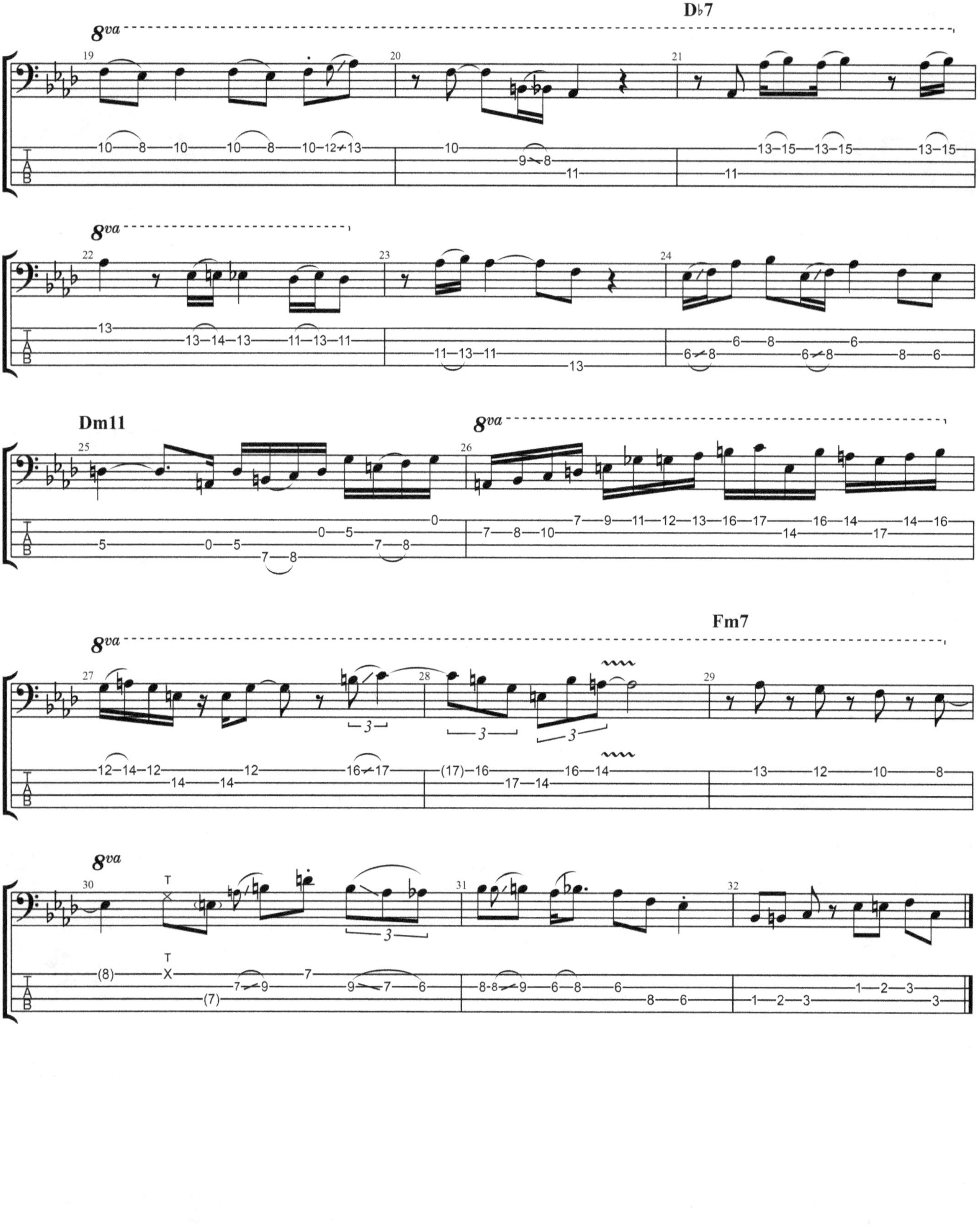
D♭7
8va
Dm11
Fm7
T
A
B

Conclusion

I hope you've gained a deeper understanding of how motifs can be used to fuel your ideas to create more engaging, melodic basslines and solos – but the learning doesn't stop here. Developing motifs as the core of your playing is a lifelong process, and one that you'll continue to refine as you grow as a musician.

I'd like to leave you with some practical things you can do to help with your musical development.

1. Practice with Intent

Motifs are all to do with repetition and variation, and you can work on developing motival ideas in your practice sessions over a groove. Start with a simple idea, just two or three notes, and explore all the different rhythmic variations and note placements you can think of. Then try adding different articulation techniques, such as slides or ghost notes. Next, move your motif into different octaves and explore it all over the fretboard.

2. Develop Motifs Over Chord Progressions

A key skill to learn is how to adapt a motif over a changing harmony. Take a simple motif – it could be a four-note cellular idea – and work on adapting it through a Major ii – V – I progression or over a modal vamp. Your goal is to adjust the shape of the motif to fit each chord, using note choices that reflect the underlying harmony. Look for ways of connecting the chord changes as naturally and musically as possible.

3. Work on Thinking in Chapters

Practice by jamming along to backing tracks and work on framing your motif development as part of a bigger musical story. Forget about focusing on individual bars for a moment, put the chord chart to one side and just use your ears. Now think about improvising over the tune using two or three chapters (or themes). Let your bottom end riffs and your soloing ideas move through a couple of themes, each of which you develop. I guarantee this will free up your playing and allow your ideas to flow.

4. Transcribe and Analyze

A great way to internalize motif-based thinking is to listen to the greats doing it and work out their ideas. Listen to musicians like Ray Brown, Jaco Pastorius, Paul Chambers, or James Jamerson, and pay attention to how they use repetition, variation, and motif-based phrasing in their lines. Transcribe some of their playing and break down and analyze the ideas they used. It will help if they are playing over a jazz standard you know well, so you can understand how they dealt with those familiar changes.

5. Jam With Other Musicians

Music is about communication and interaction, and a live jam setting is a great environment for trying out new motival ideas in a low risk setting. Often, you will come up with motif ideas that are a response to what the other musicians are playing or a reaction to the vibe you've created together. Listening is key. When you hear someone play an idea you like, get on board with it and take it further. This is where the magic happens in a band setting – those unplanned, spontaneous moments of musical serendipity.

As always, remember to have fun while playing. Every time you pick up your bass you have an opportunity to discover something new. I can't think of anything cooler!

I hope to catch you somewhere along the road.

Chris.

About the Author

Chris Minh Doky is a world-renowned bassist, bandleader, and composer who has redefined the role of the upright bass, transforming it into a bold and melodic voice. Hailing from Denmark and forged in the vibrant jazz scene of New York, Chris's distinct sound and innovative approach have earned him global recognition.

Discovered as a teenager by guitar legend Mike Stern, Chris quickly became a sought-after collaborator, joining iconic bands such as the Michael Brecker Quartet, Brecker Brothers, David Sanborn, Ryuichi Sakamoto, and the Mike Stern Band. These legendary collaborations shaped his artistry and connected him to the traditions of jazz.

As a bandleader, Chris has released numerous acclaimed albums, earning Gold and Platinum awards and a Grammy nomination, and establishing himself as a pioneering voice in contemporary music with projects like The Nomads and New Nordic Jazz.

As a composer, his works include soundtracks for films and collaborations with ballet companies such as the Royal Danish Ballet and Twyla Tharp. In 2010, Denmark's Queen Margrethe II knighted Chris, recognizing him for his contributions to the arts and making him a distinguished member of the Royal Order of the Dannebrog.

Connect with Chris

https://www.facebook.com/ChrisMinhDoky

https://www.instagram.com/chrisminhdoky/

https://www.threads.net/@chrisminhdoky

Official website + vinyl, CDs and books:

https://doky.com

www.ingramcontent.com/pod-product-compliance
Lightning Source LLC
Chambersburg PA
CBHW081438090426
42740CB00017B/3346